1

Faith & Jesus

Participant's Guide

Other Resources by Lee Strobel

The Case for Christ
The Case for Christ audio
The Case for Christ—Student Edition (with Jane Vogel)
The Case for Christmas
The Case for a Creator
The Case for a Creator audio
The Case for Creator—Student Edition (with Jane Vogel)
The Case for Easter
The Case for Faith
The Case for Faith audio
The Case for Faith—Student Edition (with Jane Vogel)
Experiencing the Passion of Jesus (with Garry Poole)
God's Outrageous Claims
Inside the Mind of Unchurched Harry and Mary
Surviving a Spiritual Mismatch in Marriage
 (with Leslie Strobel)
Surviving a Spiritual Mismatch in Marriage audio
What Jesus Would Say

Other Resources by Garry Poole

The Complete Book of Questions
Seeker Small Groups
The Three Habits of Highly Contagious Christians
In the Tough Questions Series:
Don't All Religions Lead to God?
How Could God Allow Suffering and Evil?
How Does Anyone Know God Exists?
Why Become a Christian?
Tough Questions Leader's Guide (with Judson Poling)

1

Faith & Jesus

Participant's Guide

Four Sessions on Jesus, the Resurrection, Universalism, and the
Supernatural

Lee Strobel and Garry Poole

ZONDERVAN™

GRAND RAPIDS, MICHIGAN 49530 USA

WILLOW

Willow Creek Resources

ZONDERVAN.COM/
AUTHORTRACKER

We want to hear from you. Please send your comments about this book to us in care of zreview@zondervan.com. Thank you.

ZONDERVAN.COM/
AUTHORTRACKER

ZONDERVAN™

Faith & Jesus Participant's Guide
Copyright © 2006 by Lee Strobel and Rocket Pictures

Requests for information should be addressed to:

Zondervan, *Grand Rapids, Michigan 49530*

ISBN-10: 0-310-26829-X

ISBN-13: 978-0-310-26829-1

All Scripture quotations, unless otherwise indicated, are taken from the *Holy Bible: New International Version*®. NIV®. Copyright © 1973, 1978, 1984 by International Bible Society. Used by permission of Zondervan. All rights reserved.

The website addresses recommended throughout this book are offered as a resource to you. These websites are not intended in any way to be or imply an endorsement on the part of Zondervan, nor do we vouch for their content for the life of this book.

Interior design by Angela Moulter

Printed in the United States of America

07 08 09 10 11 12 • 10 9 8 7 6 5 4 3 2

Contents

Special thanks to Ann Kroeker and Laura Allen
for their outstanding writing and editing contributions.
Their creative insights and suggestions
took these guides to the next level.

Preface

The idea came to me in the shower one morning: why not create a television program in which people of various beliefs—from Muslims to Christians to atheists to New Agers—could debate the most provocative spiritual and moral issues of the day?

What's more, prominent religious leaders could be invited on the program to be cross-examined about the stickiest questions concerning their faith.

Thanks to the vision and creativity of Jim Berger and Joni Holder, we ended up producing *Faith Under Fire*™ for a national television network. As predicted, the weekly show generated a slew of vociferous letters from viewers around the country. More than one person admitted that he found himself shouting back at his TV set.

This curriculum is based on the interviews and debates we aired on the program. You'll see knowledgeable and passionate experts discussing not just *what* they believe, but *why* they believe it. Our hope is that your group will provide a safe environment for you to be able to share your own thoughts and opinions—as well as to consider the viewpoints of others.

You'll quickly see that many of the claims made by the experts are mutually exclusive. In other words, the Christian and Muslim cannot both be right if the Bible claims Jesus is the Son of God and the Koran asserts that he's not divine but merely a prophet. One of them might be correct, or both of them could be in error, but each one of them cannot be true at the same time.

That's why we insist that our experts back up their claims. Can they defend their position logically? Do they have evidence from history or science that supports their assertions? Our task should be to determine where the evidence points.

In a similar way, the U.S. Constitution provides equal protection to all expressions of faith, and yet that doesn't mean all religious claims are equally true. According to the U.S. Supreme Court, the American ideal is to create a "marketplace of ideas" in which various opinions and beliefs can freely battle with each other so that truth will ultimately prevail.

So what is "true" about God, about Jesus, and about the afterlife? What can we know with confidence about issues of faith and morality? I hope you'll grapple with these issues in unhindered debate and discussion in your group.

One thing is true for sure: a lot hinges on the outcome.

Lee Strobel

SESSION
1

Is the
Supernatural
Real?

Read It!

Wishful Thinking?

As spotlights streak across the world-famous monument, suspense spreads among the live audience of New Yorkers gathered to witness the spectacle. With the dramatic flair of a seasoned showman, David Copperfield shocks and amazes an estimated fifty million people watching by television—the Statue of Liberty *disappears*! Go figure. Is it a miracle, magic, or a trick of the eye?

Intricate patterns and complex geometric designs mysteriously appear in farm fields overnight. Aerial photographs offer the best view of these veritable works of art created by flattened wheat and corn crops: people around the world are calling them *crop circles*. Are they alien navigational tools, electromagnetic natural occurrences, or a group of talented artists tromping around at midnight with boards strapped to their feet?

A twenty-year-old Estonian woman lost her sight after a head injury when she was a little girl. Doctors diagnosed lifelong disability. During a televised 2003 healing conference, however, she put her hands on her eyes during a service and prayed along with the leader. "When I took my hands away I was able to see!" she exclaimed. Miracle, magic, or a staged television scam?

An Arizona housewife's psychic ability to communicate with the dead helps solve crimes, piecing together complicated, confusing clues. Is it an accurate source for legitimate investigations, supernatural communication from God, satanic activity, or simply an intriguing concept for a prime-time television show?

Moses stretched out his hand over the Red Sea, and all night long a strong east wind drove the waters back and formed a path of dry land. With a wall of water on their right and left, the Israelites crossed over to the other side without getting wet—not even a single drop. Miracle, myth, a great scene for a bearded Charlton Heston, or a natural occurrence with lucky timing?

When Jesus fed a crowd of five thousand with only five loaves of bread and two fish, he looked up to heaven, gave thanks, and handed the meager food to the disciples, who in turn passed it to all the people. Everyone ate and was satisfied, and when they counted the leftovers, there were twelve basketfuls. Did the food miraculously multiply, did the disciples make it all up, or did Jesus simply inspire the crowd to pull out their hidden lunches and share what was already there?

Do miracles really happen? Or are they the exaggerated result of mere wishful thinking? This is a foundational issue to the identity of Jesus of Nazareth. To believe he's the unique Son of God who proved it by rising from the dead, we need to first believe the supernatural is possible. But is it—*really*?

Watch It!

Use the following space to take notes as you view the video in which Lee Strobel interviews Dr. J. P. Moreland, a Christian philosopher, and skeptical attorney Edward Tabash.

Discuss It!

1 Consider the following list of events: a spectacular sunset, the birth of a baby, the healing of a broken bone, a complete recovery from cancer without medical treatment, and a man walking on water. Which of these events, if any, would you label as a miracle? Why?

2 Define *miracle*. Define *supernatural occurrence*. Is a miracle a supernatural occurrence and vice versa? Explain.

3 Have you or anyone you know ever had a personal experience that you believe to be a modern-day miracle or a supernatural occurrence? Tell about that experience.

4 Why do you suppose many people find it difficult, if not impossible, to believe in miracles? What about you? Do you think it is logical and reasonable to believe a supernatural realm exists? Why or why not?

"There are two ways to look at life. One is that nothing is a miracle, and the other is that everything is a miracle."

Albert Einstein

5 Dr. Moreland outlines three strands of evidence to support the occurrence of the supernatural: "Bangs have bangers, rigged dice have riggers, and information (referring to DNA) has informers." How well do you believe these three categories of evidence support belief in the supernatural? Why?

6 Edward Tabash argues that "if there really is a banger, a dice thrower, and an informer, then such a being should not play dice with our knowledge and should be more amenable to direct experience. But we have no evidence of the types of miracles that allegedly occurred in the Bible happening today." Do you agree or disagree with Tabash's argument that if some kind of divine being—God—is real, then there should be more sufficient evidence of the occurrences of modern-day miracles? Explain your answer.

Watch It!

Use the following space to take notes as Lee Strobel continues to interview J. P. Moreland and Edward Tabash.

Discuss It!

7 Dr. Moreland claims that healings occur today. Do you agree with his statement? Why or why not?

8 To what extent do you think miracles are a product of exaggerated hope or delusional thinking? To what extent do you think miracles are genuine? Explain.

9 Dr. Moreland suggests that the mere existence of human free will is strong evidence of a realm beyond the natural realm of cause and effect. Does this line of reasoning make sense to you? Why or why not?

> "For nothing can happen without cause; nothing happens that cannot happen, and when what was capable of happening has happened, it may not be interpreted as a miracle. Consequently, there are no miracles.... We therefore draw this conclusion: what was capable of happening is not a miracle."
>
> **Cicero, *De Divinatione*, 2.28**

10 The Oxford American Dictionary defines the word *supernatural* as: "Of, or caused by, power above the forces of nature"; and the word *miracle* as: "A remarkable and welcome event that seems impossible to explain by means of the known laws of nature and is therefore attributable to a supernatural agency." Assuming that supernatural events such as miracles *do* occur—even rarely—would you say that by definition, *any occurrence* of the miraculous must necessitate the existence of some kind of divine being? Why or why not?

> "A miracle ... is an event that cannot be given a natural explanation but must be attributed directly to God, who has acted in a special way in the natural order."
>
> **C. Stephen Evans, *Why Believe?***

11 Explain why you agree or disagree with the following statement: "If God doesn't exist, by definition miracles don't happen, because a miracle is an act of God. If, on the other hand, God does exist and he is the Creator of the universe, miracles are possible because the God who created everything has the power to choose to do something else."

> "First, whatever begins to exist has a cause. Second, the universe began to exist. And, third, therefore, the universe has a cause. As the eminent scientist Sir Arthur Eddington wrote: 'The beginning seems to present insuperable difficulties unless we agree to look on it as frankly supernatural.'"
>
> **Theologian William Lane Craig**

12 Consider the purpose of miracles. John 2:23 says, "Now while [Jesus] was in Jerusalem at the Passover Feast, many people saw the miraculous signs he was doing and believed in his name." John 10:24–25 says, "The Jews gathered around [Jesus], saying, 'How long will you keep us in suspense? If you are the Christ, tell us plainly.' Jesus answered, 'I did tell you, but you do not believe. The miracles I do in my Father's name speak for me.'" According to these passages, what is the value of miracles? Even though we are twenty centuries removed from the events, how is this point still valid?

Watch It! *Lee's Perspective*

There was a time when I would have agreed wholeheartedly with Edward Tabash: the supernatural is a figment of wishful thinking. As an atheist, I ruled out the possibility of a supernatural realm. Later, though, I became more open-minded. I decided to follow the evidence of science and history wherever it pointed—even if it seemed to indicate that miracles are possible and that the supernatural exists. Based on the kind of scientific evidence that Dr. Moreland describes, as well as the convincing historical evidence for the resurrection of Jesus that I describe in my book *The Case for Christ*, I became firmly convinced that the universe is the product of a Creator and that Jesus of Nazareth is truly his Son. To me, that's the most logical conclusion I could reach. So here's my question for you: does it make more sense to deny the supernatural because of an assumption that it's impossible, or to follow the evidence wherever it leads?

Chart It!

At this point in your spiritual journey, what do you believe about miracles? On a scale from one to ten, place an X near the spot and phrase that best describes you. Share your selection with the rest of the group and give reasons for placing your X where you did.

1	2	3	4	5	6	7	8	9	10
I'm not convinced miracles occur.				I'm unsure what to believe about miracles.				I'm convinced miracles occur.	

Study It!

Take some time later this week to check out what the Bible teaches about miracles and the supernatural.

✦ Jeremiah 32:17–21, 26–27
✦ Matthew 8:23–27
✦ John 11

SESSION
2

Is Jesus a
Prophet or the
Son of God?

Read It!

Human Disguise?

Mild-mannered Clark Kent stutters and stammers through a meeting with his editor at *The Daily Planet.* When Lois Lane enters the room, he frantically fumbles his notes and nervously takes a sip of coffee. As his thick glasses slowly slide down his nose, he shoves them back using the heel of his hand, but spills hot coffee down the front of his shirt.

Moments later, as Clark is blotting the coffee stain, a change comes over his face. His superhearing has detected the screams of men and women miles away—a train's brakes have failed, and sparks fly as its wheels screech against the tracks. Hundreds of passengers are trapped as the train travels faster and faster, out of control toward a broken bridge.

Our "weakling" friend makes up a quick excuse, rushes out of the office to a nearby phone booth, and emerges as someone his coworkers would never expect: Superman!

Leaping over Metropolis skyscrapers in a single bound, he flies at supersonic speed to rescue the runaway train as it hurtles toward disaster. Seconds before the train plunges into the abyss, Superman transports the train and all its passengers safely to the other side! He even goes back and repairs the damaged track. All is well again. Superman saves the day!

What a hero!

Too bad he doesn't exist. We sure could use someone like him to intervene in our world and make things right. But Superman is the stuff of comic books and film. Nobody believes in Superman.

Well, there *are* some who believe in a superman of sorts, only they call him by a different name: Jesus Christ.

Jesus wasn't a comic book creation; his story has been around a whole lot longer than Superman's. Jesus came to us as a baby born in a manger over two thousand years ago. He grew up and developed quite a following, with people traveling alongside him from town to town. He told stories and taught lessons. Some say he was a great teacher; others claim he was a prophet, speaking the words of God to all who would listen.

But Jesus Christ had a normal side. He ate food with his disciples, drank water, got hot and thirsty and tired. Impressive as he was, he still seems weak and needy—which sounds rather ordinary and human.

Then again, the records state he turned water into wine, made blind men see, and fed five thousand people with a little boy's lunch. And as the story goes, he appeared to heal people from various diseases and even bring people back from the dead. He didn't fly, but some say he walked on water. Later, after his death, they claim he came back to life and appeared to his family and a whole bunch of friends and followers. They even argue that soon afterward, he ascended into heaven.

That sounds a lot like some kind of a superman. Did Jesus have a secret identity? Was he hiding that he was more than a human? Was Jesus really God in human disguise?

Some think Jesus was much more than a teacher or a prophet. They believe Jesus was God himself, God in the flesh. If so, he had far more than superhuman powers. If Jesus was God, he was the perfect One intervening in a history that he himself created. Divine. All powerful.

Yet unbelievable, the stuff of myths and comic books.

It would be nice, though, wouldn't it? It would be so nice to really have some kind of a superman living among us, listening for our cries for help, some kind of a hero to rescue us ... to save us.

Watch It!

Use the following space to take notes as you view the video in which Lee Strobel interviews Mike Licona, the founder of Risen Jesus, a Christian organization based in Virginia Beach, and Shabir Ally, the founder of the Islamic Information Center in Toronto, Canada.

Discuss It!

1 As a group, take a few moments to list some of the common words or phrases you have heard used to describe or define Jesus Christ.

2 When you were growing up, what were you taught about Jesus?

3 What do you believe about Jesus *today*? Is he a good man? A prophet? The Messiah? The divine Son of God? What words or phrases do you think accurately describe him? On what do you base your beliefs about Jesus?

> "Suppose, however, that God did give this law to the Jews, and did tell them that whenever a man preached a heresy, or proposed to worship any other God that they should kill him; and suppose that afterward this same God took upon himself flesh, and came to this very chosen people and taught a different religion, and that thereupon the Jews crucified him; I ask you, did he not reap exactly what he had sown? What right would this god have to complain of a crucifixion suffered in accordance with his own command?"
>
> **Robert Ingersoll, *Ingersoll's Works*, Vol. 2**

4 Shabir Ally considers Jesus to be a prophet born of a virgin, a miracle worker, and the Messiah who was raised from the dead. But he does not believe Jesus to be divine (or the "Son of God") in any way. Does Ally's conclusion make sense to you? Why or why not? Does his belief that Jesus is not divine contradict any of his other beliefs about Jesus? Explain.

5 Based on the following excerpts from the New Testament, who do you think Jesus believed himself to be? Give reasons from the text for your responses.

> The high priest said to him, "I charge you under oath by the living God: Tell us if you are the Christ, the Son of God." "Yes, it is as you say," Jesus replied. "But I say to all of you: In the future you will see the Son of Man sitting at the right hand of the Mighty One and coming on the clouds of heaven." (Matthew 26:63–64)
>
> [Jesus] said, "Do you believe in the Son of Man?" "Who is he, sir?" the man asked. "Tell me so that I may believe in him." Jesus said, "You have now seen him; in fact, he is

the one speaking with you." Then the man said, "Lord, I believe," and he worshiped him. *(John 9:35 – 38)*

Jesus answered, "I am the way and the truth and the life. No one comes to the Father except through me. If you really knew me, you would know my Father as well. From now on, you do know him and have seen him." Philip said, "Lord, show us the Father and that will be enough for us." Jesus answered, "Don't you know me, Philip, even after I have been among you such a long time? Anyone who has seen me has seen the Father. How can you say, 'Show us the Father'?" *(John 14:6 – 9)*

[Jesus answered] "I and the Father are one....Why then do you accuse me of blasphemy because I said, 'I am God's Son'?" *(John 10:30, 36)*

"For just as the Father raises the dead and gives them life, even so the Son gives life to whom he is pleased to give it. Moreover, the Father judges no one, but has entrusted all judgment to the Son, that all may honor the Son just as they honor the Father. He who does not honor the Son does not honor the Father, who sent him. I tell you the truth, whoever hears my word and believes him who sent me has eternal life and will not be condemned; he has crossed over from death to life." *(John 5:21 – 24)*

> " 'Son of Man' is often thought to indicate the humanity of Jesus, just as the reflex expression 'Son of God' indicates his divinity. In fact, just the opposite is true. The Son of Man was a divine figure in the Old Testament book of Daniel who would come at the end of the world to judge mankind and rule forever. Thus, the claim to be the Son of Man would be in effect a claim to divinity."
>
> **William Lane Craig**

Watch It!

Use the following space to take notes as Lee Strobel continues to interview Mike Licona, coauthor of *The Case for the Resurrection of Jesus*, and Shabir Ally, author of the book *Is Jesus God? The Bible Says No*.

> "The Koran does not claim to be a better historical record. The Koran reaffirms earlier historical records, namely the Gospels themselves, and it calls upon people to judge by what God has revealed in the Gospels."
>
> **Shabir Ally**

Discuss It!

6 Both Licona and Ally agree that the Gospels provide the earliest historical record of the life and ministry of Jesus Christ (written by eyewitnesses during the lifetimes of many other eyewitnesses). How reliable do you think the Gospels are as a historical source of information about the life and ministry of Jesus? Explain.

7 Licona believes there is historical evidence that Jesus claimed divinity and rose from the dead. Ally suggests that Jesus' divinity is really an idea that simply evolved over time. Who do you agree with most? Why? In what ways do the following *early* accounts from the Gospels impact what you believe about the true identity of Jesus?

> Then John [the Baptist] gave this testimony: "... I have seen and I testify that this is the Son of God." (John 1:32, 34)

> Immediately Jesus reached out his hand and caught [Peter]. "You of little faith," he said, "why did you doubt?" And when they climbed into the boat, the wind died down. Then those who were in the boat worshiped him, saying, "Truly you are the Son of God." (Matthew 14:31–33)

Jesus said to [Martha], "I am the resurrection and the life. He who believes in me will live, even though he dies; and whoever lives and believes in me will never die. Do you believe this?" "Yes, Lord," she told him, "I believe that you are the Christ, the Son of God, who was to come into the world." (John 11:25 – 27)

Thomas said to [Jesus], "My Lord and my God!" Then Jesus told him, "Because you have seen me, you have believed; blessed are those who have not seen and yet have believed." Jesus did many other miraculous signs in the presence of his disciples, which are not recorded in this book. But these are written that you may believe that Jesus is the Christ, the Son of God, and that by believing you may have life in his name. (John 20:28 – 31)

8 Licona argues that Jesus had two natures—a divine nature and a human nature. Conversely, Ally counters that "to be human means to have limitations and to be divine means to have no limitations. Jesus cannot be limited and unlimited at the same time unless he was schizophrenic?" What do you think? Was Jesus schizophrenic? Why or why not? Is it possible or impossible for Jesus to be both completely human and completely divine at the same time? Could theologians be right when they say, based on Philippians 2, that during Jesus' earthly ministry he voluntarily emptied himself of the independent use of his divine attributes? Explain.

9 Read John 20:28–31 (see reference on page 30). What do you think it would take (or what did it take) for you to come to the same conclusion as Thomas and say—as he finally did— "[Jesus, you are] my Lord and my God!" (v. 28)?

10 What are some of the implications for all of humanity if Jesus really was the unique Son of God?

11 What are some implications for *your* life if Jesus really was God in human form? Which of these implications is most difficult or troublesome to you?

"When Jesus came to the region of Caesarea Philippi, he asked his disciples, 'Who do people say the Son of Man is?' They replied, 'Some say John the Baptist; others say Elijah; and still others, Jeremiah or one of the prophets.' 'But what about you?' he asked. 'Who do you say I am?' Simon Peter answered, 'You are the Christ, the Son of the Living God.' Jesus replied, 'Blessed are you, Simon son of Jonah, for this was not revealed to you by man, but by my Father in heaven.'"

Matthew 16:13 – 17

Watch It! *Lee's Perspective*

As a skeptic, I once thought the Gospels were merely religious propaganda, hopelessly tainted by overactive imaginations and evangelistic zeal. However, my extensive investigation of the historical evidence convinced me that they reflect eyewitness testimony and bear the unmistakable earmarks of accuracy. So early are these biographies that they cannot be explained away as legendary invention. In fact, the fundamental beliefs in Jesus' miracles, resurrection, and especially his deity go way back to the very dawning of the Christian movement. Historian Gary Habermas has even found seven ancient secular sources and several early creeds concerning the deity of Jesus, a doctrine that he said is "definitely present in the earliest church." Going even further, New Testament scholar Ben Witherington III went back to the very earliest traditions, which are unquestionably safe from legendary development, and was able to show that Jesus had a supreme and transcendent understanding of himself. Based on the evidence, Witherington told me: "Did Jesus believe he was the Son of God, the anointed one of God? The answer is yes. Did he see himself as the Son of Man? The answer is yes. Did he see himself as the final Messiah? Yes, that's the way he viewed himself. Did he believe that anybody less than God could save the world? No, I don't believe he did."

Chart It!

At this point in your spiritual journey, who do *you* say that Jesus is? On a scale from one to ten, place an X near the spot and phrase that best describes you. Share your selection with the rest of the group and give reasons for placing your X where you did.

1	2	3	4	5	6	7	8	9	10
I'm very certain Jesus was an extraordinary man, but he was not God in human form.				I'm in a fog concerning who Jesus was.				I'm very certain Jesus was God in human form just as he claimed he was.	

Study It!

Take some time later this week to check out what the Bible teaches about Jesus and his identity.

+ Mark 2:1–12
+ Luke 5:20–26
+ Luke 22:66–71
+ 1 John 2:23

SESSION
3

Did Jesus Rise from the Dead?

Read It!

Really Risen?[1]

Powerful thunder cracks overhead like colossal whips. The earth seems possessed, quivering and then convulsing underfoot. Some unseen force slashes the temple curtain from top to bottom. A terrified guard shouts in awe, "Surely he was the Son of God!" For a time, darkness blankets the confusion, as if all are buried alive ...

... all except One. There is One who has breathed his last. For him, it is finished. It is finally finished. The pandemonium fades. The spectators disperse. The earth settles.

Stillness.

Silence.

Clean linen, a new tomb in a quiet garden, a huge stone. The Sabbath invites those who love him to wait, to rest. For Jesus, there is ultimate rest—from the pain, the suffering, the degradation. No more whips across the back or strikes into the face. No more beatings or bruises. The sentence has been carried out. The debt to society has been paid. It is done. It is over.

Or is it?

Early morning, the first day of the week, Mary Magdalene goes to the tomb with some other women. *But wait.* The stone is rolled back. The strips of linen are laid aside, the burial cloth folded neatly by itself. The tomb ... it's empty!

His body is gone—he's not there! Two men gleaming like lightning stand beside the trembling women. "Why do you look for the living among the dead? He is not here; he has risen!"

Risen?

---

[1] Introduction written by Ann Kroeker. Used by permission.

They rush to the disciples to tell them the news. He's risen—he's alive!—just as he had foretold. Peter and John race to the tomb and find it just as the women had said: Empty. Jesus is gone!

Where is he?

Jesus shows up everywhere. He spends time with Mary, two others on the road to Emmaus, and then Peter and the disciples. After that, he even appears to a group of five hundred. He cooks breakfast for his friends. He talks. He eats some fish. He is very much alive. They still wonder, *Is it really true?*

"Why are you troubled, and why do doubts rise in your minds?" he asks them. "Look at my hands and my feet. It is I myself! Touch me and see; a ghost does not have flesh and bones, as you see I have." They still find it hard to believe despite their joy and amazement! *It can't be ... can it? Can he really and truly be alive?*

Yes, it's him! Without question, this is his body. The marks of the crucifixion are still evident: the nail-punctured hands and feet, the pierced side. How can he be alive after all that physical torment? How can he be walking around, talking with people, eating a broiled fish?

He patiently extends an invitation to Thomas, the doubter, "Put your finger here; see my hands. Reach out your hand and put it into my side. Stop doubting and believe."

Thomas does. The doubter touches, sees—and believes. "My Lord and my God!" Thomas exclaims, convinced that this is Jesus, the One he saw crucified, dead, and buried. And the One who rose again on the third day exactly like he said he would. Now here he is, healed, though scarred, and standing alive before them all.

So, the dead hero comes back to life. How about that—a storybook ending! Everyone's delighted! At least Jesus and his friends are. And that's that, right? All's well that ends well. Close the book and move on.

Right?

Watch It!

Use the following space to take notes as you view the video in which Lee Strobel interviews Dr. William Lane Craig, one of the world's leading authorities on the resurrection, and Richard Carrier, an ancient history scholar and atheist.

Discuss It!

1 Before you watched this DVD segment, what did you believe about the resurrection of Jesus? How was your view of the resurrection impacted by the segment? What questions did the segment raise for you?

2 William Craig lists five facts he believes point to the resurrection of Jesus as an actual event in history:

- Jesus of Nazareth was executed by crucifixion under Roman authority on the eve of Passover.
- Jesus' corpse was then laid in a tomb by Joseph of Arimathea, a delegate of the Jewish Sanhedrin that condemned Jesus.
- The tomb of Jesus was found empty on the Sunday morning following the crucifixion by a group of his women followers, including Mary Magdalene.
- Thereafter, various individuals and groups of people saw appearances of Jesus alive from the dead.
- The original disciples suddenly and sincerely came to believe in the resurrection of Jesus despite having every predisposition to the contrary.

Do you think these facts are sufficient pieces of evidence to support the resurrection as an actual event in history?

> "In a profound sense, Christianity without the resurrection is not simply Christianity without its final chapter. It is not Christianity at all."
>
> **Theologian Gerald O'Collins**

3 Richard Carrier argues that the empty tomb was first described in symbolic terms and later became misinterpreted as an actual event. Do you agree with Carrier's thinking? Why or why not?

4 Do you agree or disagree with Carrier's idea that if God really wanted to save all of humanity, he would not have sent his message of salvation "only in secret, to only a few people, only one time, two thousand years ago"? Explain your answer.

5 If God really did send Jesus into the world to be our savior, what are some ways he could have made that unmistakably clear to everyone, but didn't? How would these ideas have impacted what people believed and didn't believe about Jesus?

Watch It!

Use this space to take notes as Lee Strobel continues to interview Dr. William Lane Craig, a research professor of philosophy at Talbot Seminary and author of *The Son Rises*, and skeptic Richard Carrier, author of *Sense and Goodness Without God*.

Discuss It!

6 Read the following eyewitness accounts from the New Testament of the post-resurrection appearances of Jesus:

> Then the eleven disciples went to Galilee, to the mountain where Jesus had told them to go. When they saw him, they worshiped him; but some doubted. (Matthew 28:16–17)

> When Jesus rose early on the first day of the week, he appeared first to Mary Magdalene, out of whom he had driven seven demons. She went and told those who had been with him and who were mourning and weeping. When they heard that Jesus was alive and that she had seen him, they did not believe it. (Mark 16:9–11)

> Later Jesus appeared to the Eleven as they were eating; he rebuked them for their lack of faith and their stubborn refusal to believe those who had seen him after he had risen. (Mark 16:14)

> While they were still talking about this, Jesus himself stood among them and said to them, "Peace be with you." They were startled and frightened, thinking they saw a ghost. He said to them, "Why are you troubled, and why do doubts rise in your minds? Look at my hands and my feet. It is I myself! Touch me and see; a ghost does not have flesh and bones, as you see I have." When he had said this, he showed them his hands and feet. And while they still did not believe it because of joy and amazement, he asked them, "Do you have anything here to eat?" They gave him a piece of broiled fish, and he took it and ate it in their presence. (Luke 24:36–43)

> Early in the morning, Jesus stood on the shore, but the disciples did not realize that it was Jesus. He called out to them, "Friends, haven't you any fish?" "No," they answered. He said, "Throw your net on the right side of the boat and you will find some." When they did, they were

unable to haul the net in because of the large number of fish. Then the disciple whom Jesus loved said to Peter, "It is the Lord!" As soon as Simon Peter heard him say, "It is the Lord," he wrapped his outer garment around him (for he had taken it off) and jumped into the water. The other disciples followed in the boat.... When they landed, they saw a fire of burning coals there with fish on it, and some bread. Jesus said to them, "Bring some of the fish you have just caught." ... Jesus said to them, "Come and have breakfast." None of the disciples dared ask him, "Who are you?" They knew it was the Lord.... This was now the third time Jesus appeared to his disciples after he was raised from the dead." (John 21: 4–10, 12, 14)

For what I received I passed on to you as of first importance: that Christ died for our sins according to the Scriptures, that he was buried, that he was raised on the third day according to the Scriptures, and that he appeared to Peter, and then to the Twelve. After that, he appeared to more than five hundred of the brothers at the same time, most of whom are still living.... Then he appeared to James, then to all the apostles, and last of all he appeared to me also. (Paul in 1 Corinthians 15:3–8)

What is your reaction to these verses? Why do you think some of the actual witnesses to Jesus' resurrection had difficulty believing even their own eyes?

> "It was therefore impossible that they [the early Christians] could have persisted in affirming the truths they have narrated, had not Jesus actually risen from the dead, and had they not known this fact as certainly as they knew any other fact."
>
> **Simon Greenleaf, an authority in jurisprudence at Harvard Law School**

7 Assuming the biblical accounts above are accurate, does Craig's claim that the *diversity* of the resurrection appearances negate the possibility of the "hallucination theory"? Why or why not?

8 According to the following Scripture, what kind of evidence did it take for Thomas to believe that Jesus had risen from the dead? In what ways can you relate to Thomas? What kinds of evidence would it take for *you* to believe that the resurrection occurred?

Now Thomas (called Didymus), one of the Twelve, was not with the disciples when Jesus came. So the other disciples told him, "We have seen the Lord!" But he said to them, "Unless I see the nail marks in his hands and put my finger where the nails were, and put my hand into his side, I will not believe it." A week later his disciples were in the house again, and Thomas was with them. Though the doors were locked, Jesus came and stood among them and said, "Peace be with you!" Then he said to Thomas, "Put your finger here; see my hands. Reach out your hand and put it into my side. Stop doubting and

believe." Thomas said to him, "My Lord and my God!"
Then Jesus told him, "Because you have seen me, you
have believed; blessed are those who have not seen and
yet have believed." (John 20:24–29)

9 How would your beliefs about Jesus Christ be impacted if it were proven that Jesus never rose from the dead? Do you believe that the Christian faith hinges on the resurrection?

10 In your opinion, what is the significance of the resurrection? Does it matter to you that Jesus rose from the dead?

> "I know pretty well what evidence is, and I tell you, such evidence as that for the resurrection has never broken down yet."
> **John Singleton Copley, one of the greatest legal minds in British history**

"If Christ has not been raised, your faith is futile; you are still in your sins."

Apostle Paul in 1 Corinthians 15:17

11 What implications does the resurrection have for you? For example, how would your view of life, death, and the afterlife change if the resurrection has or has not occurred?

Watch It! *Lee's Perspective*

The evidence for the resurrection was pivotal in my decision to become a Christian. First, there's the empty tomb—everybody in the ancient world acknowledged it was vacant. The question was: how did it get empty? The authorities made up the absurd story that the disciples stole the body, but they clearly lacked motive or opportunity. Second, there are eyewitnesses. More than 515 individuals encountered the risen Jesus, and hardcore skeptics like James and Saul of Tarsus were transformed into believers. As British theologian Michael Green said, "The appearances of Jesus are as well authenticated as anything in antiquity.... There can be no rational doubt that they occurred." Third, there are early accounts that date back so close to the events that they cannot be the product of legendary development. And, fourth, there's the willingness of the disciples to die for their conviction that the crucified Jesus came back to life. They didn't just *believe* the resurrection was true; they were in a unique position to *know* firsthand that it actually occurred. Nobody knowingly and willingly dies for a lie. To me, the bottom line was this: anybody can claim to be the Son of God, but only Jesus proved it by conquering the grave.

Chart It!

At this point in your spiritual journey, what degree of certainty do you have that the resurrection actually occurred? On a scale from one to ten, place an X near the spot and phrase that best describes you. Share your selection with the rest of the group and give reasons for placing your X where you did.

1	2	3	4	5	6	7	8	9	10
I see no evidence for Jesus' resurrec- tion.				Some- thing very unusual happened back then, but I'm not sure what.					I believe Jesus rose from the dead as the early church claimed.

Study It!

Take some time later this week to check out what the Bible teaches about the resurrection.

+ Mark 16:1–14
+ Luke 24:13–53
+ John 20:10–31
+ John 21

SESSION
4

Do All
Roads Lead
to God?

Read It!

One Way?

Jeff and Tony sat on the floor of their dorm room, staring at the open books in front of them.

"So ... what do you make of this, Jeff?" Tony asked.

"I don't know," Jeff muttered. "I didn't like it when you told me about it, and I don't like it any better reading it for myself."

"I know what you mean. You got another slice of pizza over there?"

"Here," Jeff slid the box over to his friend, the remaining piece of cold pepperoni pizza shifting during the transition. "Maybe it's not as bad as it sounds. Let me read it again." He picked up the Bible and read the troubling verse carefully: " 'Jesus answered, "I am the way and the truth and the life. No one comes to the Father except through me." ' Nope, it still sounds totally exclusive. I hate it."

"It doesn't sound like the gentle, loving Jesus that I remember hearing about growing up," Tony said.

"It seems like he's drawing a line in the sand. You're either in or out," Jeff complained.

"But ... what if that's it? What if he *is* the way, the *only* way?" Tony asked as he munched a bite of pizza.

"Look, maybe we've got it all wrong. Maybe it doesn't mean what we think it means. We need an expert," Jeff said.

"What time is it?" Tony asked, polishing off the last bite of crust.

"Late," Jeff observed.

"Let's just check out that church down on Third. Maybe somebody will still be around there."

"Why not?" Jeff agreed.

The door creaked as they slowly pushed it open. The pews were empty, the lights dim, the wooden floors echoed as they walked down the aisle. A moment later, someone in the back opened a door, spilling a ray of light into the sanctuary.

"Can I help you guys?" asked the slender, gray-haired man standing in the doorway.

"Yeah, sure, that would be great," Tony said as he introduced the two of them. "We were talking about a verse in the Bible, and we wanted another opinion. What do you make of this?" Tony flipped open his Bible to John 14:6 and read it aloud. "That sounds awfully exclusive. It doesn't seem fair to me to count some in and some out based on whether or not they happened to hear about Jesus."

The pastor—"just call me Stephen"—nodded; he had taught from this passage a few times in his thirty-plus years of ministry. "Jesus didn't mean he was the *only* way," he assured them. "He meant he was the *best* way. He was—and is—the *best* way to learn about the way to God."

Jeff shook his head. "But that's not what it says. Jesus is saying he is *the* way, and we need to find truth and life through him alone. Isn't that the point he's making?"

"Imagine taking a road trip to Chicago," Stephen began. "There are a lot of different highways and side roads you could take to get there. Some ways would take longer than others, but there *is* a best, most direct way. The best way is the most efficient way, but it's okay if you don't take the most efficient way, because all ways will eventually get you there." Stephen noticed Tony tapping the arm of his chair nervously. "What's on your mind, Tony?"

Tony stopped tapping. "I see your point, but some things *are* very narrow. Jeff's car runs only on gasoline, not water or milk or beer. We can't try pouring Mountain Dew in his gas tank because there's no other way to make his engine run so we can make the trip to Chicago in the first place. See, there's no give or take on some things. Look, Stephen, a lot of times, there really is only one way ... and maybe this time, Jesus meant he was *the* only way."

Stephen looked at the boys with compassion. He understood their desire to find answers. It reminded him of his own search years ago, which led him into ministry. He wanted to encourage them. "Think about it—"

"I am!" Tony exclaimed. Jeff elbowed him.

"No, it's okay. I understand your excitement. Let me try explaining it this way. In science, the answers are often cut-and-dried, but in subjects like philosophy and theology, it's more interpretive, more fluid. So consider this: If you want to master a subject, say something like physics, you have a couple of ways to go about it. You could go to the bookstore and the library and gather a lot of books around you, read them all, and you'd probably learn a lot about physics. But another way," he leaned forward, hoping this analogy fit the undergrad mentality, "would be to sign up for a college course on physics taught by a brilliant professor. Now, you tell me, which of those two ways would be the *best* way to learn about physics?"

"Signing up for the course," Tony answered.

"Exactly." Stephen watched their faces. "That's what Jesus meant. Going to God through Jesus is like taking the course taught by the all-knowing master. He isn't the *only* way to God, but he *is* the *best* way."

Both Tony and Jeff hesitated, each deep in thought. Finally, Jeff broke the silence. "Thanks for your time, Stephen."

"No problem. Come back any time. Take care."

When the heavy door shut behind Jeff and Tony, they paused on the top step. "What's the matter, Jeff?" Tony asked.

"I don't know ... I guess I just wonder," Jeff continued, as they headed back to the dorm. "It still seems like he's changing the meaning. Hey, which way do you want to take back to the dorm?"

"I don't suppose it matters," Tony said with a grin. "Or does it?"

Watch It!

Use the following space to take notes as you view the video in which Lee Strobel interviews Kenneth Bowers, a member of the national governing body of the Baha'i of the United States and author of *God Speaks Again: An Introduction to the Baha'i Faith*, and Gregory Koukl, president of Stand to Reason and author of the book *Relativism: Feet Firmly Planted in Mid Air.*

Discuss It!

1 Why do you think there are so many different religions in the world? Is it confusing or frustrating to you that there are so many religions from which to choose? Explain.

> "The soul of religions is one, but it is encased in a multitude of forms.... Truth is the exclusive property of no single scripture.... I cannot ascribe exclusive divinity to Jesus. He is as divine as Krishna or Rama or Mohammed or Zoroaster."
>
> **Mahatma Gandhi**

2 Why do you think God allows so many religions to exist? Why doesn't he just narrow down the choices so it's easier to find him?

3 Do you think all the major religions are fundamentally the same or fundamentally different? If you can, give reasons to back up your answer.

> "I am absolutely against any religion that says that one faith is superior to another. I don't see how that is anything different than spiritual racism. It's a way of saying that we are closer to God than you, and that's what leads to hatred."
>
> **Rabbi Schmuley Boteach**

4 What is the difference between the following two statements: "There are many different ways to get to my house."/"All roads lead to my house." Are both of the above statements logical? Why or why not?

5 How likely does it seem to you that any one religion would have the final say on what is true or not? Explain.

> "To overlook obvious differences between religions might seem broad-minded. In reality it is about as proud and narrow as a person could get. To say all religions are basically the same is to claim to be smarter than each of the billions of people who believe the unique aspects of their religion are of supreme importance to God. It is to claim that even though you are not an expert in their religion, you know they are wrong—you know their religion is really no different."
>
> **Grantley Morris**

> "The extreme [Christian] who believes that all Muslims go to hell is probably not so much ignorant . . . as blinded by dark dogmatic spectacles through which he can see no good in religious devotion outside his own."
>
> **Theologian John Hick**

6 Kenneth Bowers holds to the Baha'i belief that there is one God who has progressively revealed the same path through various divine messengers throughout history (including, but not limited to, Buddha, Jesus, and Muhammad). What are some of the strengths and weaknesses of this claim? Do you agree or disagree with this assertion? Explain.

7 Given two contradictory and opposing statements, choose all that apply:

❏ Both statements may be true at the same time.
❏ Both statements cannot be true at the same time.
❏ At least one statement must be false.
❏ One statement may be true or both statements may be false, but both statements cannot both be true at the same time.

> "Moses could mediate on the law; Muhammad could brandish a sword; Buddha could give personal counsel; Confucius could offer wise sayings; but none of these men was qualified to offer an atonement for the sins of the world.... Christ alone is worthy of unlimited devotion and service."
>
> **Theologian R. C. Sproul**

8 Gregory Koukl makes the following statement: "Either Jesus was the Messiah or he was not the Messiah. If he's *not* the Messiah then the Jews are right and the Christians are wrong. If he *is* the Messiah then the Christians are right and the Jews are wrong. Under no circumstance can they both be right. When you die you either go to heaven or hell, or you get reincarnated, or you get absorbed into God, or you lie in the grave. But you can't do them all." What is your reaction to Koukl's statement? Does it seem reasonable to expect all religions to be true in their own way, in spite of significant differences? Why or why not? Explain your response.

Watch It!

Use this space to take notes as Lee Strobel continues to interview Kenneth Bowers and Gregory Koukl.

Discuss It!

9 How does the legend about the elephant and the blind men apply to the issue of searching for and discovering the truth about God and religion? Do you agree with its conclusion? Why or why not?

An Indian Legend
"Six Blind Men and the Elephant"

It was six men of Indostan
To learning much inclined,
Who went to see the Elephant
(Though all of them were blind),
That each by observation
Might satisfy his mind.

The First approached the Elephant,
And happening to fall
Against his broad and sturdy side,
At once began to bawl:
"God bless me! but the Elephant
Is very like a wall!"

The Second, feeling of the tusk,
Cried, "Ho! what have we here,
So very round and smooth and sharp?
To me 'tis mighty clear
This wonder of an Elephant
Is very like a spear!"

The Third approached the animal,
And happening to take
The squirming trunk within his hands,
Thus boldly up he spake:
"I see," quoth he, "the Elephant
Is very like a snake!"

The Fourth reached out an eager hand,
And felt about the knee:
"What most this wondrous beast is like
Is mighty plain," quoth he;
"'Tis clear enough the Elephant
Is very like a tree!"

The Fifth, who chanced to touch the ear,
Said: "E'en the blindest man
Can tell what this resembles most;
Deny the fact who can,
This marvel of an Elephant
Is very like a fan!"

The Sixth no sooner had begun
About the beast to grope,
Than, seizing on the swinging tail
That fell within his scope.
"I see," quoth he, "the Elephant
Is very like a rope!"

And so these men of Indostan
Disputed loud and long,
Each in his own opinion
Exceeding stiff and strong,
Though each was partly in the right,
They all were in the wrong!

John Godfrey Saxe (1816 – 1887)

10 Do you agree or disagree with the concept that because human understanding is finite, and God is infinite, humans need some kind of divine revelation to more fully understand who God is, so that we are no longer like the "blind men" only seeing a small part of the larger truth? Explain your response.

11 According to the following Bible verses listed below, do you think that Jesus taught that there are many paths to God? Explain.

> [Jesus speaking] "Enter through the narrow gate. For wide is the gate and broad is the road that leads to destruction, and many enter through it. But small is the gate and narrow the road that leads to life, and only a few find it. Watch out for false prophets. They come to you in sheep's clothing, but inwardly they are ferocious wolves." (Matthew 7:13 – 15)

> For there is one God and one mediator between God and men, the man Christ Jesus, who gave himself as a ransom for all men — the testimony given in its proper time. (1 Timothy 2:5 – 6)

> Therefore Jesus said again, "I tell you the truth, I am the gate for the sheep. All who ever came before me were thieves and robbers, but the sheep did not listen to them. I am the gate; whoever enters through me will be saved. (John 10:7–9)

> [Jesus] was in the world, and though the world was made through him, the world did not recognize him. He came to that which was his own, but his own did not receive him. Yet to all who received him, to those who believed in

his name, he gave the right to become children of God. (John 1:10 – 12)

There is a way that seems right to a man, but in the end it leads to death. (Proverbs 14:12)

Jesus answered, "I am the way and the truth and the life. No one comes to the Father except through me." (John 14:6)

Jesus answered: "Watch out that no one deceives you. For many will come in my name, claiming, 'I am the Christ,' and will deceive many.... At that time many will turn away from the faith and will betray and hate each other, and many false prophets will appear and deceive many people." (Matthew 24:4 – 5, 10 – 11)

12 According to the Scriptures above, what conclusions can you draw about Jesus' claim to be the only way to God? How confident are you that all roads lead to God?

"Even though many religions seem to be the same on the surface, the closer one gets to the central teachings, the more apparent the differences become. It is totally incorrect to say that all religions are the same."

Josh McDowell, *Answers to Tough Questions Skeptics Ask about the Christian Faith*

13

How do the exclusive claims of Jesus worry, bother, or embarrass you? How has your reaction changed over time? Explain.

I can certainly understand Ken Bowers' desire to interpret world religions in a way that diminishes their distinctions and downplays Jesus' claims to exclusivity. However, I agree with Greg Koukl—there are irreconcilable differences at the very foundations of the world's faiths. To give just three examples, polytheists believe there's a multiplicity of impersonal gods; Christians believe in one triune and personal God, with Jesus as God's only Son; Muslims specifically deny God's triune nature and Jesus' divinity. To gloss over these differences is to gut these religions of their essential beliefs. To me, Jesus' teachings are clear: he is the only way to God. Otherwise, his death on the cross would have been superfluous. The issue, then, becomes whether we can believe Jesus when he makes this remarkable claim. And that's where Jesus' credentials become important—his miracles, which were seen by eyewitnesses, including skeptics; his fulfillment of ancient prophecies against all mathematical odds; and his resurrection from the dead, which authenticated his claim to be the Son of God. In short, I believe Jesus backs up his identity unlike the leader of any other world religion. And that's what gives him unique credibility when he says he's the sole path to salvation.

Chart It!

At this point in your spiritual journey, do you believe religions are fundamentally the same or fundamentally different? On a scale from one to ten, place an X near the spot and phrase that best describes you. Share your selection with the rest of the group and give reasons for placing your X where you did.

1	2	3	4	5	6	7	8	9	10
I believe all religions are basically the same.				I'm not sure it's a good idea to even try to compare religions with each other.				Other religions may have some truth, but they are all very different.	

Study It!

Take some time later this week to check out what the Bible teaches about various religious points of view.

+ Matthew 7:13–27
+ Matthew 22:1–14
+ Matthew 25:31–46
+ John 3:16
+ John 14:6
+ 1 John 5:20